MIA ADELMAN

FLIPPING HOUSES

The Ultimate Guide on Flipping Houses for Beginners, Learn the Basics As Well As Insider Secrets On How You Can Turn Trash Houses into Cash

Descrierea CIP a Bibliotecii Naţionale a României
MIA ADELMAN
    FLIPPING HOUSES. The Ultimate Guide on Flipping Houses
for Beginners, Learn the Basics As Well As Insider Secrets On
How You Can Turn Trash Houses into Cash / Mia Adelman. –
Bucharest: Editura My Ebook, 2020
    ISBN

MIA ADELMAN

FLIPPING HOUSES

The Ultimate Guide on Flipping Houses for Beginners, Learn the Basics As Well As Insider Secrets On How You Can Turn Trash Houses into Cash

My Ebook Publishing House
Bucharest, 2020

MIA ADELMAN

FLIPPING HOUSES

The Ultimate Guide on Flipping Houses for Beginners.
Learn the Basics As Well As Insider Secrets On How You
Can Turn Trash Houses Into Cash

A... Book Publishing House
Bucuresti, 2020

TABLE OF CONTENTS

WHAT IS LEVERAGE AND WHY USE IT

Making the Most of Fixer Upper Leverage

When starting out in a fixer-upper business, you will first have to consider many things. It is never indicative to success to jump into any business venture prematurely and without proper planning. You will first have to learn as much as you can about the business before jumping on the bandwagon.

Depending on how your business is financed, buying and selling these properties may involve very little or a lot of money. One good way to leverage your interests is to employ the use of other people"s money and resources.

Most people think that success in this field of business involves a lot of hard work. Yes, hard work is an essential element to success in this field. However, knowledge is also important. And if you are to succeed, you will need to use your wealth of knowledge to the limit.

An example of how good strategies can help your success is to understand how leveraging can make dealing with fixer uppers profitable and easier on the budget.

The truth of the matter here is that you can get other"s money to work for you. You can earn more without plunking your cash in as investment. While it seems counterintuitive - who, in his right mind, would ever hope to get good returns on investments when he or she hasn't put in any investments at all, one must think – it truly is possible to get other people"s money, time, and expertise to work for your own benefit.

Using Other People"s Resources

One way to think of OPM (Other People"s Money) working for your benefit is think how most people expect to make earnings from fixer upper ventures.

First off, most people would want to purchase the property itself. They could do this through a couple of ways. They could purchase the land out of their savings or take out loans to pay for the property.

This method, while good in itself, has some limitations. If you use your savings to buy property for a venture – and for some unforeseen reason, the venture goes bust and you are unable to sell the property, then you may have practically thrown your life savings out the window.

You can make other people"s money work for you here. For example, what if you take a 95% seller"s financing plan. This means you only pay for around 5% of the property"s value. Then, you proceed to lease the area to tenants. The money you make from the rentals can be used to pay for the loan.

In the end, theoretically speaking, you would have only paid 5% cold cash for the property, and made the property itself – with the help of its tenants – pay for the property the rest of the way. If the property costs $100,000, then that means you only pay $5,000 to own the property after some time – with extra income to boot. Not a bad proposition now, is it?

This is, in effect, having other people pay for something you will own in the future, and is one of the smart ways to make investments.

You could also use other people"s resources such as time and expertise when trying to make money from fixer upper homes. For example, if you aren't well-versed in renovating properties, why not have other people do it, and make a profit at the same time.

How? Take for example a home that is sold by a distressed owner – house unkempt, needing repairs. Now, as a fixer upper yourself, the first thing you would want to do is think of how you can purchase and renovate the place, and then sell it on the market.

But what if, instead, you make plans to purchase the property and then show the property to other fixer uppers who may want to the take the property from your hands and do the hard work of renovating and selling the property on the market.

You can then sell the property again to this partner and have them renovate and sell the property. Just don"t forget to take your profit from the pay you will be asking of them for the property! This, in technical terms, is called flipping.

If you look at it closely, you will have had made somewhere close to what most people in the same business make without even having to do the hard work required of them – remodeling, renovating, and marketing.

The technique there, however, is that you will have to be aware of how to choose potentially great properties. If you have an eye for that then it won"t be much of a problem.

If you do this, you will have effectively used other people"s expertise and time in helping you make a good profit. This is a great way to leverage other"s assets to work for your advantage.

DETERMINE YOUR GOAL

What is Your Goal? Setting up a Realistic Fixer Upper Venture

In the real estate business, a fixer-upper can be a smart way to get started in the business and earn good money at the same time. Buying and selling fixer-uppers, when done with discretion and with good buying judgment, can prove to be a good way to earn money without having to invest heavily – especially when done right.

When starting out in a fixer-upper business, you will first have to consider many things. After learning what you can, then proceed to drawing realistic expectations and plans to put your business into action. From here, you can then set goals and work on plans to meet those goals. While fixer upper business is attractive, high-income ventures, if not done properly, can drive one into serious debt if not done properly.

What is a Fixer Upper?

For those unacquainted with the term, fixer uppers is real estate bought from distressed home owners, fixed up (hence the term fixer upper) and sold at premium prices. In a way it is like finding a jewel in the rough, polishing it, and sending it back to the market for a good price.

Many have gone on to be millionaires from this kind of venture. If you look at it, theoretically, it makes a lot of sense. However, no matter how attractive it may seem to be, this type of business isn't without its risks.

Fixer Uppers involve a lot of money, assumptions and risks. You assume that the real estate you are buying can be fixed up and sold at a higher price. You also assume that the house can be brought up to a state where it is attractive to those seeking a home to move into.

If you put all these intangibles together, you will find that the risk may be a little too high for some people. In fact, this is the reason that these ventures are high-profit ones, they are also high risk.

You can, however, reduce this risk by doing good background studies, setting realistic goals, drawing up good plans, and making calculated risks. Here are some good tips on building a good fixer upper business venture.

1. Goals – You will have to set realistic goals for your business. Fixer upper homes can earn a good deal of money, but it wouldn"t hurt to set a conservative figure as you learn the ropes. Sometimes conservative is good – especially when you are just starting to get the hang of a venture.

Some people set unrealistic goals, like aiming for $100,000,000 at the onset, hoping against all hope they can make and sell at an incredible rate. However, it would be better to keep with a realistic figure. Most fixer uppers will agree that $100,000 is a good amount to expect per year in a fixer upper venture.

This figure is taken by considering the sale of 5 fixed up houses with a cut of $20,000 per house. This isn't a bad figure to start with. And you will be able to adjust better figures as you learn more about the business.

You will also have to consider what this business will mean to your life. Will you give up your day job just to focus on this business? Will you do this on your own free time? Or will you try a little of both to see where you do best?

2. Properties – Make sure you don't put all your eggs in one basket. This could lead you to losing more than you are willing to in one venture. Depending on your source of financing, you could handle one or more properties at a time. Again, it will be advisable to start slowly before gradually increasing the number of properties you handle at one time.

3. Sell or Keep – Some fixer uppers will decide to fix and keep, instead of fix and sell. This is not folly, but shouldn't be performed without prior thought. If, with your research, you learn that the property rates for a given land ameliorate pretty quickly per annum and that you stand to earn more if you hold the property for a while, then do so.

If you see that you don't stand to earn much by keeping it, then put it on the market as soon as you see fit. On the other hand if you notice that prime property is creeping towards the property you are fixing up, holding on for a while might not be such a bad idea.

FINDING THE RIGHT AREA

How to Find the Right Area for Fixer Uppers

A Fixer Upper business venture could very well be your way out of the 9-5 day job. Not only does it hold the possibility of earning more, it also gives you a good opportunity to manage your own time, travel and meet new people. Plus, the extra money doesn't hurt.

Those that have become rich as a result of fixer uppers testify to the fact that while it can be a little risky, especially at first, it could be well worth the sacrifice and the risk. It is a very attractive, well-earning business with a very good rate of return.

Depending on how your business is financed, buying and selling properties may involve either very little or a lot of money. One good way to leverage your interest is to employ the use of other people"s money.

Any successful fixer upper will tell you that the secret to success is the knack to find good properties that are seemingly un-sellable, but when fixed up can actually fetch more than its weight in gold. While some have an almost preternatural ability to nose up such properties, there are ways that everyone can learn to sniff out good property buys.

1. **Doghouses** – the term doghouses come from homes that aren't structurally damaged, only unkempt and needing cosmetic upkeep. Some homeowners have good sound homes but neglect to do simple things such as clean the confines, plaster the wall with paper, and keep the roof in good repair and such.

These houses may be in such a condition because the owners are both lazy, in dire financial straits and unable to maintain their homes, or planning on moving anyway. In such a case you will want to inspect the home closer, you could be in for a pleasant surprise.

If you spot such a house, you will do well to investigate more since you have, in front of you, a good chance of snagging a diamond in the rough.

Owners of such houses find it hard to sell these houses even if there is only minimal damage. This is because they are unattractive and people tend to have the inability to look beyond minor faults to find a good sturdy house standing in front of them.

2. **Look at the Neighborhood** – Do a little research on the neighborhood to find out if the area is a booming area worthy of prime property prices. Some properties, no matter how wonderful they may look like, can't fetch good prices because they are in bad neighborhoods, or are in areas that are underdeveloped.

Ask around the neighborhood for signs of improvement in the last few years. Check out the amenities of the area, the community support, and the general impression of other people on the neighborhood.

Good house hunters are able to catch a good neighborhood on the rise, just along the time when property space is cheap and right before the area experiences a boom in property prices. Other things to ask about are crime rates, accessibility, proximity to hospitals, schools, and other community fixtures.

3. **Ask the Mayor** – If you have contacts, it would be nice to know the government"s plans for the area. If the government plans to develop the area, create higher class amenities and

housing then there could be a sudden surge in the prices in the area. This is then a good time to catch the wave before prices skyrocket.

You could also research plans for companies and consortiums to develop malls, transportation, and other facilities. These could radically affect the prices in the area. If you are able to anticipate this ahead of time then you are in line to make good money from this business.

4. **Crime** – Crime and community is a major factor in the choice of a home. Make sure that the properties you put your sights on have low crime rates and have a strong sense of community. This means that the people in these areas should get along with each other. This is a very important aspect of the choice of home for most people.

WHERE TO OBTAIN FINANCING

Where Do You Get the Money for Fixer Uppers?

For most people, seeking financing for fixer upper ventures will prove to be one of the hardest things to consider. Some of those that have been able to save up might consider plunking in their savings into such a venture.

However, this would be tantamount to putting all your eggs in one basket. If you lose the basket, there goes your future. And that would be financial suicide, by any measure.

If you are looking for good financing schemes for your fixer upper here are a few good alternatives.

1. **Housing Loans** – The US Department of Housing and Urban Development 203 (k) rehabilitation mortgages is one of the best solutions if you are looking for a single, low-interest solution to purchasing and fixing up a home property with one

loan. This is a great alternative to taking out multiple higher interest loans that could cripple your finances – you can instead have just one loan that is decidedly easier to pay off.

While this is a great alternative to other loans and mortgages, it does have guidelines. For one, it is subject to guidelines submitted by the Federal Housing Administration – these guidelines may also vary from state to state.

For example in order to be eligible for this loan, it has to have improvement costs of at least $5000 for a one to four condominium or family residence unit. After eligibility, the loan then becomes available with wonderfully low interest rates for terms as long as 30 years!

And to top this, you will only have to pay about 3 percent down payment if you are an owner or occupier, and 15 percent if you are an investor. It is also available is you want to finance the repair not only of properties you don't own yet, but properties that are already in your fold as well.

2. **Other lending instruments** – You could also use any number of lending instruments available to you. Mortgages or second mortgages are common among those that purchase fixer uppers. Some also pay visits to their banks for loans.

In some cases, seller financing provides a better alternative to other loans. Other property managers themselves can finance the purchase of their own property, with you plunking down as little as 5 percent of the total price. This method is more amenable to people than having to pay the whole thing out of their own pocket immediately.

In any case, on should find a financial instrument that is acceptable and payable in agreeable terms since not all available financing options are practical or useful for your purpose. You should keep a look out for low-interest, long-term loans that are available.

Of course, such attractive loans are only available on certain conditions. And to get the better deals, you will have to fall under attractive brackets.

3. **Getting Better Loans** – If you want nice, low-interest, long-term or short-term financing, you will have to be an attractive client to most banks. For you to fall under the „attractive client" bracket, you will have to have your financial house in order.

If you have bad credit history – having debts left and right and defaulting on previous loans, then you will probably have trouble getting good loans. For such dire situations, the only opportunities that present themselves at this point will be high-interest loans.

While some people will be glad to have someone offer a loan at this rate, you should always remember that every percent counts. And that every percent could very well spell a few more hundred or even thousands of dollars in payments yearly. You, in the eyes of lenders will have become a high-risk client, which warrants the increase in interest you will be experiencing.

The best way to get attractive loans is to get your financial house in order before setting out for available financing. Without such measures, you will end up with financing that may be too hard to handle.

In a nutshell, the best way to get into the good graces of the lenders is to pay off existing debts (or to at least settle with previous lenders for a payment plan), and to avoid getting into new debt immediately.

There are many forms of financing available, each with its own idiosyncrasies. Study all the terms of these loans before entering into them and learn how each one fits your current financial situation before considering any one of them.

BUYING BELOW MARKET VALUE

The Truth about Buying Homes below Market Value

Buying homes today can be a very expensive undertaking. Nevertheless, it can also bring highly valuable and priceless assets.

With the growing market value of most homes, alleged home specialist say that people should think about their lenders first before they even think about buying their homes. In this way, you can estimate and foresee what kind of home you can afford.

This can literally make a good implication of something positive. However, lending money doesn't always provide 100% guaranteed satisfaction. It has its drawbacks and you will always be the one on the losing end.

For this reason, some experts provide more sensible advice such as buying homes that are below the market value. You may not be aware of it but it is possible that you can buy your home below market value. Yet, it doesn't necessarily mean that buying a home below market value is the best solution to today''s skyrocketing prices.

Buying homes below market value requires guts, strength of mind, and patience to get the best deal. Keep in mind that there is a very strong reason why these kinds of houses are being sold below market value. And most often than not, these reasons aren't something you should be happy about.

Buying a fixer upper home is one of the best targets if you really want to buy a home below market value. These kinds of dwellings are usually being sold on the market at very low prices because of their structural and cosmetic defects.

Fixer upper homes aren't all bad. In fact, you can fix them up and live comfortably like the others, but you still have to consider the cost of expenses you have to take when fixing a fixer upper home.

However, there are other factors that you have to keep in mind before deciding on buying a fixer upper home. Here are some of the factors you have to consider as well:

1. Market condition

Buying homes below market value like fixer upper homes may not be good enough if the market condition is at its worst. This means that if you plan to make a profit out of the present value of your fixer upper home and suddenly the market condition has turned bitter, the idea of buying homes below market value may not sound good after all.

Keep in mind that home market values are constantly decreasing in values. If this is the case, buying homes below market value such as fixer upper homes may bring you problems instead of profits. Even if you have placed substantial investments on home improvements but the market condition is bad, buying homes below market value may not bring you benefits.

2. What you know about home improvements

If you don't have any knowledge about home improvements, buying a home below market value is useless. Why? It is because you can't clearly say that you have made a good buy if you will be spending more than what is necessary. You might just overdo it.

Overlooking the things you need to improve in your fixer upper home can decrease its value. Bad improvements are just as bad as not having to improve it at all.

3. Mathematical analysis

Not all cheap items make good buys. If you really want to see good results out of buying a home below market value, you should know how to mathematically analyze the present and expected estimated values. These things will help you assess if your fixer upper home is really worth your money.

4. Research skills

Buying homes below market value isn't possible without good research skills. You should be skilled enough to conduct extensive inquiries and exploration about the available homes that are being sold below market value to get the best deals.

Houses may still vary even if they are all below market value. It is important that you know how to find the best one with the lowest price.

Indeed, the possibilities of finding and buying homes below market value are endless. However, it is imperative that you know these factors to get the best value even if you are getting a cheap buy.

PREPARATION

HOW TO GIVE A FIXER-UPPER THE PERFECT MAKEOVER

It"s not only ugly ducklings that get makeovers. These days, even houses are in need of image renovations. In real estate lingo, fixer-upper is the term used to describe a house in need of remodeling or repair. Buying and selling fixer-uppers can be a sound investment…if you follow our tips below.

DON"T FALL IN LOVE AT FIRST SIGHT

Remember that beauty is in the eye of the beholder. So a house that seems absolutely wonderful to you doesn"t necessarily mean it"s similarly perceived by others. Choose a fixer-upper that appeals to your mind, heart and pockets! Avoid choosing one with a market value that"s equivalent to your total budget. If you do, you"ll have no money left for repair and you

27

might end up with a home that sells lower than its original and expected value.

REMEMBER THE 4 R"S

Let"s say that you"ve already chosen a fixer-upper to buy and you"re just waiting for the deal to close. In the meantime, take a tour of the house and try to identify its flaws.

Keep the 4 important R"s in mind as you walk from room to room – remodeling, repairs, renovating and refurbishing. Each one is different from another and there"s a chance that you might make use of all of them later on. It"s better to be prepared beforehand so you know how to allocate your budget appropriately.

GET AN EXPERT

Unless you"re a real estate expert yourself, it"s better to hire a qualified individual for a day and ask him which aspects of the house should be repaired or modified in some way. Accompany him from room to room and write down everything he says. Don"t hesitate to ask questions because keeping mum at the wrong time may prove to be a costly mistake later on!

It"s very important to be able to get a full structural survey of the house while you"re with your hired expert. The survey shall serve as your guideline or blueprints when you start reinstating the house to its original beauty.

GET ANOTHER EXPERT

A fixer-upper may not benefit from the expert eye of a real estate professional. It must also be looked over by other experts before it can be fully judged as functional and sellable.

Start with an electrician. Ask him if each and every outlet is currently working and if the house has any faulty wiring. If it"s presently without any electricity, ask the electrician how much it would cost to have the house wired. If you"re particularly concerned with the environment, you can also ask the electrician to survey the house and have him tell you what you can do to make it an energy efficient home.

Lastly, get an engineer to view the house. With the trail of disaster left by super hurricanes still printed indelibly in our minds, you can"t blame homeowners if they express concern about the stability and the foundation of the home. Ask the engineer to estimate up to what magnitude on the Richter scale the house is able to survive.

TAKE PHOTOS OF EVERY NOOK AND CRANNY

You can never be too sure that you haven"t overlooked anything about the house. And since you can"t bring your investment home, the next best thing to do is take as many photos as you can of each room of the house. Take at least four photos for every room (one for each side). Remember to set the size of photos to its maximum capability.

Take an extra memory card just in case you run out of memory. This way, you"ll be able to study each photo in full-blown detail. Get a friend to look over the photos with you because four eyes work better than two.

CHECK WITH YOUR ACCOUNTANT

The last thing you should do is set up a meeting with your accountant, financial advisor, bank manager or whoever it is that gives you advice about your finances. Explain the present state of the house and leave no stones unturned. Seek their wisdom and ask specifically up to how much you should be willing to spend on the house and how much to sell it for.

Keep these tips in mind and you"ll surely end up with a beautiful swan of a home!

IMPROVING THE INTERIOR

How to Avoid Ho-Hum Interior Design Changes

Next to the outdoor appearance of a home – what it looks like up front and when you"re standing outside the gate – the next most important thing that will weigh heavily on a prospective buyer"s mind is the interior design. You need to make the most out of the first encounter between the upper-fixer you"re selling and the client. You need to make them exclaim WOW and not make a ho-hum-boring sigh!

Repainting the Walls and Ceilings

Walls usually dominate and set the tone for any room. That"s why it"s important to choose the right paint or wallpaper when renovating any room or home. Painting is less costly than having new wallpaper upholstered and since upper-fixer renovations are frequently subject to budget constraints, painting is ultimately your best option when it comes to changing how the walls appear.

Always use a primer or base coat when painting walls. Make sure that the primer"s color matches the surface paint color of the wall to achieve a beautiful blending and layered effect. Using a primer will also help save money because it often makes a second coat of paint unnecessary.

If it"s your first time repainting walls and ceilings, don"t hesitate to ask for tips from the people working in hardware stores. You should know that certain types of paint brushes work better for certain types of paints. Foam brushes, for instance, are great when used to apply simple touch-ups. Never paint on a wall or ceiling that needs fixing. Have them repaired first before applying a fresh coat of paint.

Choosing one color for the entire home will again help you stick to your budget because all you need to purchase is the primer and the surface paint color. If, however, you wish to make use of varying colors, keep in mind that different colors and textures produce different results. Matte or flat finishes for walls are better able to hide any of the walls" imperfections. Glossy finishes, on the other hand, are able to reflect more sunlight. Cool shades like blue and green – water hues, in other words – are said to give rooms a cooler atmosphere while hot shades like red, yellow and orange can make rooms warmer than it is.

How to Maximize Space

Most clients – if not all – love spacious homes and this is why it"s important for you to maximize space in the fixer-upper you"re planning to sell, especially if it"s of limited size. If your budget permits it, consider adding windows to your house because they create the illusion of added space. Mirrors have a similar effect as well but you should be careful with where you plan to place them. Look for any part of the house that"s "under-used". If the kitchen has more than enough storage space, you could turn the pantry into a bathroom. The area under the staircase is often overlooked; consider turning it into a storage closet or a small bathroom.

Tackling the Dirtiest Parts of the House

The kitchen and the bathroom are considered by many as the dirtiest parts of the house because a lot of activities often take place in these areas. And since use of water is mostly involved, these rooms often have muddied and moldy appearances. Consider making changes to the walls and floors that would give them better protection against the damaging and other unappealing effects of exposure to water. Using dark colored tiles in bathrooms, for instance, will easily make dirt and mud less visible. In the kitchen, consider using laminated countertops because they are more durable and absolutely easier to clean.

Cleaning and Polishing as the Finishing Touches

When all is said and done, the last thing you should do in preparation of having prospective clients come over for an open-house is to give it the benefits of a general cleaning session. No speck of dust must be left in any part of the house. Polish the floors, the banister, the window rails and every door knob in the house. A clean house will always give a better impression than one that"s beautifully designed but neglected.

Hiring a Contractor

Lastly, don"t be afraid to ask for help if you need it. Hiring a contractor may mean paying extra fees but this decision can help you avoid more costly mistakes!

KITCHEN REMODELING

How to Make an Upper-Fixer"s Kitchen Working and Spanking Cool

Kitchens are one of the busiest parts of the house. Many things go on in the kitchen and this is why it"s often the dirtiest, most abused and most in need of repair in the whole house. If you"re planning on investing in an upper-fixer, be sure that one of your top priorities will be renovating the kitchen.

How Do You Plan on Marketing the House?

Before you touch even one object or take one brick out of the kitchen, consider first how you plan on marketing the house. Consider the house"s size. Consider the neighborhood. Is it more suited to become a family home, an apartment or a bachelor"s pad? The answer to this question will enable you to learn as well what type of kitchen would be best to use or create.

A bachelor"s pad, for instance, would only need a simple but functional kitchen – if the kitchen area is too big, you should consider making the area smaller if your budget allows.

A family home, however, would need lots and lots of space in the kitchen because this is one of the communal spots of the house and where everybody gathers for some quality family time.

How Much Are You Willing and Able to Spend?

Keep in mind that those questions are completely different but you have to reach a compromise between the answers to both questions. It"s more difficult to save money when redesigning or renovating a kitchen than a bedroom. There are more accessories available to make a bedroom or even a living room more beautiful for a relatively small amount. Kitchen accessories, however, are comparatively limited and only few of them are priced cheaply.

Consider Giving the Kitchen a Facelift

Take a critical full structural survey of the kitchen. Take snapshots of every corner of the room. Try appraising it with an unbiased eye. Is it in need of major repairs or is it only in need of a makeover and a fresh new appearance? If it"s the latter then maybe all it needs is a simple facelift. A facelift involves making superficial changes, nothing major or anything that would require you to spend loads of money. Facelifts include but aren't limited to removing old wallpaper, re-applying varnish to kitchen cabinets, laminating countertops and changing faucets.

Are There Any Time Constraints?

If, for any reason, you are subject to time constraints, you need to consider this while making remodeling plans for the kitchen. How long do you think it will take you to accomplish your plans? If you are in need of contractors, have them give you an estimate on the number of days they need in order to complete their job. If you are going to order materials or supplies, ask how long it will take to deliver them to your home.

Give your project at least one week"s allowance for delays or problems. If there"s a possibility that you won"t be able to meet the deadline, consider altering some of your plans for the kitchen or asking for an extension of the deadline.

Space Planning for the Kitchen

If you believe that there"s need for changes beyond simple repair and facelift, you should also consider the present layout of the kitchen and see if it allows people to move and work in comfort.

Kitchen Cabinet Area – Is there truly enough space for kitchen equipment, kitchenware, cleaning materials, canned goods and other miscellaneous kitchen items?

Vertical Space – Don"t neglect using vertical space to your advantage. If the kitchen area is small, making use of vertical space for kitchen cabinets will prevent the layout for being too cluttered.

Staying on the Dot

You need to make full use of each day you"re given when remodeling the kitchen or the house in general. Make a list of the repairs you need to accomplish for the kitchen to resume functionality. Don"t postpone for tomorrow what you can do today.

Remember: no matter how much you wish to redesign the kitchen into the most beautiful culinary center in the neighborhood, you still have to consider your budget. You still have to remember that this is an investment and the need to save as much money on repairs as possible.

MAJOR BATHROOM REMODELING

Major Bathroom Remodeling Guidelines

Although the bathroom, compared to all the other rooms in the home has the smallest area, a "major bathroom remodeling" can be costly; in fact can be compared to renovating a small house.

Upgrading your bathroom appliances as well as knocking down walls is generally the scope of "bathroom remodeling" jobs. You will need important help that will include a designer or architect, an electrician, plumber, carpenter, professional tile setter and possibly also a "general contractor" to organize jobs and bring everybody together.

For the superlative bathroom remodeling results, you need to contact a contractor because this won't be a simple do-it-yourself remodeling project.

Benefits of hiring a contractor

The most notable benefit of obtaining the help of a contractor in your major bathroom remodeling project is acquiring "peace of mind" and having to deal with just one person to impart your ideas to or to blame in case something goes wrong.

A reliable contractor carries with him the knowledge and skills to supervise and manage everything in the bathroom remodeling process starting from the tearing-out phase up to the installation of the last plumbing piece.

Your contractor coordinates with the plumber, electrician and any other workers needed in your bathroom remodeling project, obtains all essential permits demanded by your city and organizes work schedules in order that no time is wasted.

Design and planning

A collection of architectural and design plans will help not only you but your bathroom remodeling professionals as well visualize the completed project, although any design ideas and preparations may be helpful.

When contemplating major remodeling on your bathroom, the most essential thing to keep in mind is to consider and look into your "bathroom remodeling" project estimate or figures as well as what you imagine is the most attractive bathroom design for you.

Throughout the your bathroom remodeling course, remember to think and look of the remodeling project from all angles such as functionality, overall design, aesthetic appeal, comfort, materials and colors.

While you may avoid crazy designs generally in other rooms of your house, your bathroom can deal with vibrant patterns and colors and whimsical themes. Furthermore, it can be a meticulous depiction of your homes ambience.

Consult a designer for bathroom design suggestions and ideas, let them know of your design preference so they can give you a sketch or you can examine magazines and cut out designs, ideas and photos that correspond or match with what design you have in mind.

Here are basic questions that you should ask yourself to help you design your bathroom:

- What do you want to accomplish?
- Which do you prefer more, sink or counter space?
- Do you need one more shower compartment?

- Would you like to put in a whirlpool or spa setting?
- Do you need lots of cabinets or just open shelves for storage space?

Establishing a realistic budget for your major bathroom remodeling

When determining your bathroom remodeling budget, bear in mind the bathroom design inspiration and ideas you like as well as if they are expensive.

Remember, it is less expensive when you don't relocate your bathroom"s plumbing fixtures, like sinks or toilets, so then when you have a much smaller budget, incorporating your present bathroom plan into your new bathroom design can in fact, be very economical.

Furthermore, the cost of your bathroom remodeling project will greatly depend on your choice of fixtures and the quality of bathroom appliances you would like to have. Some bathtubs, fixtures and even tiles could be expensive because of their brand names.

Considering that you can spend hours in your bathroom, it is very important that you give thorough consideration on how you want to use your bathroom.

Today's bathroom is no longer just a place for taking a bath, brushing your teeth, etc. It now can a place where you can relax in the tub, light a candle and read a book and just take pleasure in its calming ambience.

Bathrooms need to be just as functional, good looking and comfortable as the other rooms of your home.

Enjoy the excitement and fun of your bathroom remodeling project and take pleasure in the many years of contentment and gratification offered by your finished bathroom project.

ELECTRICAL, PLUMBING AND HEATING

Fixer Upper: A Home Inspection Professional Is Essential To Identify Major Plumbing and Electrical Defects

Fixer uppers are homes that usually need a moderate number of home repairs generally not requiring special knowledge or expertise on your part, as the homeowner.

Fixer upper homes can be excellent bargains when the "asking price" is significantly lower than comparable homes nearby but in good or excellent condition.

A fixer upper needing a cosmetic fix-up can be a great property. They generally need some repainting outside and inside (paint can do a lot of wonders), floor refinishing or new carpets, new lighting fixtures, little repairs, complete cleanup and landscaping.

If the home necessitates massive repairs such as electrical and plumbing problems that usually are expensive, it will slash your profit back or worst, eliminate it.

Before purchasing a house you believe is an effortless fixer upper, a professional home inspection should be considered because the inspector can provide you an accurate idea of what existing problems the home has and what repairs are needed as well as an approximate repair cost.

Here are frequently found fixer upper defects that might need your attention:

- Roofing
- Insulation
- Plumbing system
- Electrical system
- Central heating
- Central cooling
- Water seepage
- Structural

These defects requires expensive professional repair especially when talking about the value these repairs will return upon resale.

Most often, these major defects go unnoticed because fixer-upper buyers usually can't see the inside workings, hidden out of view behind walls or covered inaccessible areas that are often taken for granted.

Cracked "heat-exchanger" in the heating system, faulty wiring, termite damage and safety and health problems like lead accumulation, water pipes as well as asbestos insulation are common physical flaws that you can't see immediately.

Indications of these hidden problems are as follows:

• Moisture stains that can be found on ceiling and walls could mean plumbing problems.

• Separations between wall and floor specifically for outer walls could mean structural problems.

• Sawdust piles near woodwork or wall corners can be an indication of termites.

A home inspection from a professional

A professional home inspection can cost about 200-325 dollars depending on the kind of property, location, square footage, etc.

When hiring a professional home inspection of fixer upper houses, it is wise that you obtain quotations first from several competing companies. However, the lowest bidder shouldn't be immediately given the job; aside from the price, you must inspect the "quality of service" they offer as well as the company name. It is important to choose a company with a good reputation.

Several home inspection companies have some kind of computer-like machines which can supply inspection reports and descriptions instantly then the company adds their "pre-printed" sections which are very helpful for you in order to understand the fundamentals of repairing, fixing and replacement.

Furthermore, home inspection companies supply an entirely impartial appraisal and assessment of the house, inspecting everything carefully from electrical systems, and plumbing to structural to make certain that the fixer upper house you are purchasing is sound.

Professional home inspectors can make certain that all major systems (air conditioning, plumbing, and furnace) are working properly or they can pinpoint defects to you because these kinds of repairs will cost you a great deal of money.

However, do keep in mind that major repairing problems don't automatically indicate that you shouldn't purchase the fixer upper home, because they can and should be added in the home"s price negotiations.

A good fixer upper seller or realtor will and can factor in said considerations or concerns and you possibly can purchase the home for even less if you put it clearly that you will be responsible for the repair or replacements. Just be careful that you don't get tricked. Never take anybody''s word that the plumbing, the furnace or the electrical have no problems at all; you have to make certain.

Sometimes you can easily "walk away" from an excellent fixer upper home deal in a terrible neighborhood. At times, when you can specifically pin point what repairs and replacements are necessary, you can obtain a substantially lower price.

The trick in fixer upper homes is to discover those necessary repairs because often, the home seller won't point those out to you.

SIMPLE FIXER UPPERS

Tips on Giving Your Fixer-Upper an Efficient Makeover

It"s easy to remodel any fixer-upper. If you don"t have good taste on interior design, you can simply hire an expert to take care of renovations for you. What makes it particularly hard is when you have a budget to stick to and an investment that"s on the line.

Step One: Planning for Changes

This is the first step in remodeling your fixer-upper. No project would be smooth sailing without proper and organized planning. If there"s no need to hurry, you should take your time studying and analyzing each aspect of the house before doing any physical changes or modifications.

Consider Weather Conditions

Is the location an area that"s particularly favored by firestorms, typhoons, hurricanes or floods? If so, you should ensure that your house is weatherproofed against these natural calamities. If not, make a list of the things that should be repaired or changed and estimate the costs for each item on the list. These problems must be fully addressed because of your personal safety as well as that of your family are involved.

Windows and Doors

Don"t underestimate the overall effect that small but numerous changes can bring. The simple change in windows and doors can easily enhance the beauty of any home. Get rid of damaged or antique window treatments and make use of new ones. Consider using aluminum blinds because they are durable and come in varying colors. There are also other types of window treatments available to fit your budget so make sure you choose one that fits the overall design of your home.

Secondly, consider the present state of the doors. Creaking doors are creepy and not fun so consider replacing old ones with new but stylish substitutes.

The Small Overlooked Items

Check if each and every faucet in the house is working. If there"s only one that"s not working, you should try a faucet that matches the others still in use to maintain uniformity. If there are multiple faucets that aren't functioning, consider changing them all.

Test out all the electrical sources in the house. Switch on and off every light and find a replacement for everything that doesn"t work. Check the outlets as well and have broken ones replaced.

Are any parts of the roof leaking? Subject the ceilings to a thorough appraisal. You can ask an expert to help you out. There is nothing more undesirable than a leaking house. It makes the poorest of impressions – a reaction that you should avoid at all costs.

Step Two: Implementing the Changes

Set a Deadline and Budget Limits

The longer it takes for your fixer-upper to be remodeled, the more money you may lose. Use a project management tool to help you achieve your goals on time but without going over your budget.

DIY, Contractual Work or a Compromise?

Work immediately on the aspects of the house that can be easily repaired with Do-It- Yourself projects like painting the walls, reorganizing furniture if there are any and other simple repairs. If there is anything that"s beyond your capabilities, hire a contractor right away. Forcing yourself to accomplish things that you aren't equipped to do may cause the damage to worsen.

Tips on Hiring a Contractor

Hiring fees for contractors vary so be sure that you choose one that fits right with your budget. Set up an initial meeting with the contractor and see if there"s a meeting of the minds. Avoid hiring a contractor who believes his opinion always counts more than yours. Be sure that your contract includes terms and conditions that address cases of delays on project completion that are through no fault of your own.

Don"t Let Stress Get to You

Repairing a fixer-upper can sometimes be extremely stressful. If all you can accomplish for the day is just giving yourself more headaches, call it quits and take a breather. Rest for one full day and you"ll find your energy level back to normal upon returning to work.

Step Three: Analyzing the Results

You"ve done everything you can to make the fixer-upper as comfortable and as presentable as it can be. Step back and take a critical look at what you"ve accomplished. If you still have money and time left, consider refurbishing the house as well or spending money on more extensive advertising. If you think you have it made, give yourself a pat on the back for a job well done. Congratulations!

IMPROVING THE EXTERIOR

By improving the exterior you can sell a fixer-upper!

The saying you broke it, you fix it can somehow apply to the business of buying and reselling property. Only this time, it"s you buy it and you fix it.

One of the first areas a buyer of a house will notice when checking out property is the exterior. It is the task of the landscape architect to make the garden top notch and appealing for a possible client.

Similar to that of the engineer and the building he constructed, a landscape architect envisions the planning, design, rehabilitation and preservation of the man-made property, such as in this case, real estate or simply fixer upper homes.

Hiring professionals to assist you in the landscaping of the property"s exterior maybe costly, that is why if you can do it by yourself, why not? Here are some guidelines that may assist you in improving the landscape"s exterior.

1. Make the best out of curb appeal

Now there"s something aesthetically appealing with a downward slope portion of the ground when checking out a garden. It"s simple but landscaping on slopes isn't an easy task.

First, you need a retaining wall. Think of it like you"re getting retainers after years of wearing braces. A retaining wall assists in preventing erosion.

You can build your own stone-retaining wall. All you need are a mason"s hammer, shovel, garden hose and a couple of stakes.

Terrace the slope by building retaining walls that could hold the soil in two or more places. A mortar-less retaining wall comes in with a drainage system which means water seeps through the cracks between the stones. However, when damage from such water pressure takes place, it can easily be repaired.

Choose stones that have two flat sides which will be placed atop the retaining wall. The heavier the stones, the more stability it will provide. The heavier the stones, the greater work you"ll have to do lifting it. It"s for the best anyway.

For your wall to withstand external pressure, dig a trench about eight to ten inches deep, fully submerging the first row of stones. Check that the stones are leveled. Just because it is a downward slope doesn"t mean the stones should be jagged when lined up. After completing the first layer of the foundation, continue with the next course of stones. Tuck in soil when there is a gap in between the terraces. Cascading plants such as lobelia and thyme are also appealing when planted in stone retaining walls.

2. Cleaning out and replacing flower beds

Of course, even plants need a fresh start. In landscaping, it is also advisable that plants get replenished. Treat the weather like it is spring and you"re about to embark on a change, so that"s why you clean out the flower beds.

Remove the dead foliage from the past seasons. Make sure that the flowers are given enough fertilizer and water to be replenished again. The flower bed soil must be healthy so that the nutrients will be taken in by the plants.

By replacing flower beds, make sure that the flowers you will purchase and plant are those that are in tune with the season. Ask a flower expert about the right care for the plants.

It is also advisable that the cleaning extend not only up to the flower beds but also to the lawn. A green, lush healthy garden is always something that captures the attention of a possible buyer.

3. Maintaining the lawn

What could be one of the hardest tasks in bringing out the beauty of a garden yet again is the lawn. First step you must do is to get the right type of grass to plant. Afterwards, purchase the fertilizer and ask the plant specialist when it is advisable to fully water the lawn.

Getting a gardener to maintain and water the lawn once a week will help in improving the lawn"s beauty to the onlooker"s eye. Make sure to get someone who you can trust, who will do the job efficiently and quickly with an asking price that won't be a hassle for you to shell out.

Some landscape architects also consider providing xeriscape to the exterior. This is where the retaining wall comes in. When done correctly, then erosion and the unwanted water can be suppressed from coming in and destroying the plants in the garden.

It is the landscape architect"s job to improve the exterior of a buy-and-sell house just as it is an architect"s job to improve the interior. Just like when you"re checking out someone you see in the bar, the physical appeal also matters.

WINDOWS - ROOF – FENCING

A fixer upper house has to have pretty windows and more!

After checking out the exterior of a home, the possible client then goes in and checks the interior. The furniture is regarded as accessories of a house, but it is the other crucial stable points in the house - such as the windows, roof, fencing, patio and porches - that provide the foundation and must also be taken a look at.

When it is a fixer-upper home, it is the seller"s task to replace parts of the house that needs replacing. That may be costly but it is an investment that is wisely done and compensated afterwards.

Like the rule often applied in life, why let someone do it, when you can do it yourself?

1. Window

Check if the window needs repainting or new glass. If they do then make sure that the measurements are accurate so as to not waste time, effort and money in putting in newly-bought glass to the window"s structure, only to find out that it doesn"t fit.

Brush the glass clean to make it attractive for the possible buyer.

The difference between repairing to replacing the window is the acquired cost. If you are to repair the window, it would cost less than if you have it entirely replaced. If you believe that you have enough skills to repair the window yourself, then just get the materials and do the work hands-on. If not, call your nearest window provider and assist them by giving them the dimensions of the windowsill.

2. Roof

When you first see a fixer-upper house, check if there are leaks in the roof. Signs would be possible mold and/or stagnation seen on floor. Constantly wet floor that is resulted from the ceiling"s drip would leave brownish or yellowish marks. These are found on the edges of the floor.

This is hard work if you are to repair it yourself and is costly if you have someone replace it for you. This is a job that is often left to the experts. Carpenters pretty much know the 411 on roof foundations and when they are called in, not only will they patch up the holes on the roof, they"ll also check if the roof is infected by termites and other unwanted colonies that ruin a house"s foundation in time.

3. Fencing

What"s a good garden if fencing is blah? It helps to present the fixer-upper house at its finest, inside and outside. So from the windows to the roof, we head back to the garden and check out fencing.

This can easily be done on your own. Walk to your nearby handy-store and purchase the needed wiring that would highlight the garden. If the fences need to be painted, go. It"s always better to get a new set - something that shows starting anew.

If you are replacing the fence on your own, check if the lines are straight and not crooked. One jagged area may be a turn-off for a possible buyer. It is all about presentation.

4. Patio

Everyone needs a place to relax. Patios can never be overlooked in a fixer-upper house. When repairing the patio area, check if the patio set is still usable. If not, replace them by buying new ones. Make sure that the design goes well with the room.

What is important in the patio is the atmosphere. You must be able to enter and unwind. Check if appliances have to be bought such as little centerpieces you could put on the table or vases for flowers. Candles are also an option.

Double check if the ventilation is alright. If not, then consider your options in revamping the room for airflow.

5. Porches

Just like the garden, the porch also needs to be checked out. The porch is the welcoming party of the entire house. A porch must be inviting for the possible buyer. Therefore, it is advisable that the texture of the porch is comfortable and relaxing. Some houses even have swings. It"s always up to the owner what kind of porch he prefers.

The important thing is the porch is one of the first things a buyer sees.

As mentioned earlier, repairing or replacing these areas of a fixer-upper house may be strenuous and costly, but who knows what the end product will result to? There"s a possibility that you could sell the property double the price you paid it for or better yet, re-think of selling it and just keep it for yourself!

BUY, FIX IT UP AND RENT

Renting Out a Fixer Upper: Things to Consider

Fixer Upper real estate can prove to be a very good business as long as you make the right decisions and put your money in the right places. One of the major decisions you will have to make when dealing with a fixer upper is what to do with the home once you have purchased the property itself.

You could either resell it at a higher price, flip it –meaning you resell the house immediately to other fixer uppers who would like a crack at fixing the house up and selling it on the market, or you could have it put on the market as a property for rent.

Here are a few things you should know regarding fixer upper homes so that you can make a better decision considering whether a property should be put up for rent instead.

The Advantages

The great thing about investing in rental houses is that well-placed homes can appreciate pretty quickly depending on the neighborhood. If you happed upon a fixer upper home in a suddenly progressive community, you could have very well hit the jackpot.

Looking at the bigger picture, experts predict that most properties appreciate in value by only about five percent per year. That doesn't sound very promising, does it? However, the amount you earn from a rental home isn't solely dependent on the appreciation in value of a property.

Even if you plunk down about $100,000 on a home, you could still make good income by the use of leverage. Leverage is the use of other people"s money, expertise, and time to purchase a home or make an income out of one.

This is made possible by the fact that you don't have to purchase a home right out of your savings. That would be a great risk to take – what if your venture tanks?

Fortunately, not too many fixer uppers purchase property this way. Most fixer uppers use some sort of loan or financing to get their hands on potentially juicy property.

After using that method to finance your purchase, you will of course, have to make regular payments to lenders plus interest. Now, what if you purchase a home like this, fix it up, and let it out for rent, and then use the rental money you get to cover loan payments and get an income as well?

That would be a great way to make good income out of the situation and is a great way to use leveraging.

It is also possible to refinance after a previous fix up so that you can move on to other properties. You should never rush the issue. Make sure you have ample time to make sure a property is ready for rental and can make an income before making the next move.

However, if you are confident in your skills as a fixer upper, having dealt with it in the past, then you may juggle a bit depending on your skill.

Having said that, the reason you should be careful not to commit to too many properties at the same time is the fact that some properties may earn a negative cash flow. This means that the property doesn't earn its keep, making leveraging impossible. You will end up paying the loans out of your own pocket.

This is a sure way to go broke fast – especially if you have multiple properties that are tanking at the same time. If you aren't able to plug this gap immediately, you could find your pockets hemorrhaging hard-earned cash!

Negative cash flow is caused when the rent doesn't cover the loan payment plus interest. It may be that the tenants don't pay on time, or the units are vacant, or the rent can't be made to justify a large loan payment.

To avoid the two later problems make sure you choose a good location in progressive areas. This will help assure you that you will have an ample supply of tenants. Also you will have to hone your landlord skills to the hilt to deal with those that skip paying up.

This skill involved keeping good records of transactions, tenant information and such. You will need this information to both deal fairly and legally with issues that arise out of the lease.

Buy, Fix It Up and Sell

Selling a Fixer Upper: Tips and Techniques

If you have considered fixing up and selling property with the intent to sell instead of renting, then here are some invaluable tips that should fall on any ear hoping to make positive income on all properties they plan to sell.

1. The First Impression – Those that shop around for homes will give you about fifteen minutes for you to impress them. If you aren't able to bring a twinkle in their eyes during this period then you may have lost the fight.

You then should be able to make the best presentation a fifteen minute talk can give. Rehearse all the good things you know about the home. Enumerate first all pertinent information they may want to know about the home and the neighborhood.

Among the most important things to enumerate are the availabilities of the various basic utilities and amenities available in a home. Water supply and engineering, gas lines, structural design all have a place in your presentation.

Also help them experience how wonderful living in such a place would be. Walk them through a day where the house meets all their needs. You could also tell them about the neighborhood and advantages of the place.

If the area is near schools, malls, hospitals, and institutions, let them know. This is one of the most important considerations home seekers look for in a home. They don't want to be stuck with a pretty home that is so far out in the plains that travel becomes an inconvenience.

If travel will become a burden to them, then coming home will prove to be a bigger one too.

You should also be ready for pretty much any question a home owner can throw at you. Make sure you do your research and learn as much as possible about the house and its structure. This will give you leverage when taking about the home you are trying to sell.

Also it wouldn"t hurt if you treated the home as your own. You should carry the demeanor of one that is sorry to have to part with such a great property.

2. Choosing an Agent – For a fixer upper, choosing a good agent may prove to be one of the hardest and most exasperating tasks at hand. However tiring it may be, it is still necessary. Remember that a good real estate agent can make the property business smoother for you, especially if you are new to the field.

When looking for a real estate agent, ask them and yourself the following questions. How long have they been in this line of work and how many sales have they been able to generate per year. This is a good gauge of a real estate agent"s skill and aptitude.

Also, ask the agent any question you can think of regarding your fixer upper property. If they can answer adeptly and without batting an eyelash, then they have above average communication skills and knowledge of the field.

Communication skills are very important in a real estate agent. You should be able to trust your agent with your work without having to worry if you are both on the same page. Good communicators are also better sales facilitators and can make your job a lot easier – not to mention more profitable.

Also take a peek into their sales plans and the method they use to lure in sales. This will at least placate you with the thought that they know what they are doing.

3. Make the Fix up worth it – With a good agent and a good pitch talk, you will then have at least good property to show. You, by now, must have purchased a home with is only in need of cosmetic and external repair. If this is so, pour in the effort to make the home worth the money.

A good way to make a rough estimate is to look at other existing homes on the market similar to the one you are selling. Make sure, however, that you are able to make a profit by taking into consideration the house value, fixing fee, insurance, and other expenses you may have incurred while dealing with this house.

Printed by Libri Plureos GmbH in Hamburg, Germany